The Lord of the Sword and his Lady

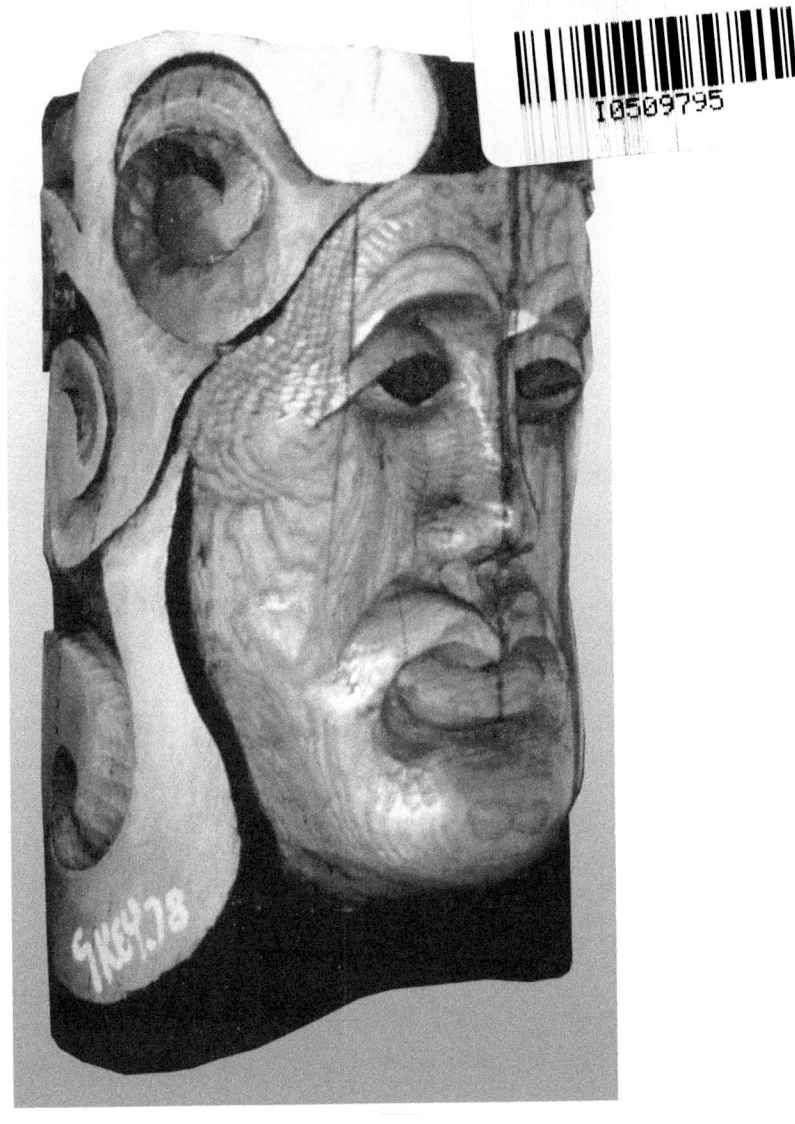

Maxine Handy

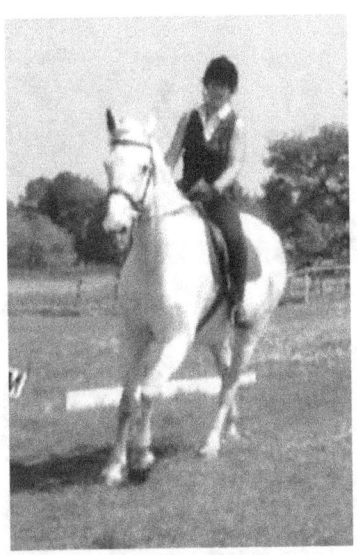

Eleanor on Bluestone

"And the youth pricked forth upon a steed with head dappled-grey, of four winters old, firm of limb with shell-formed hoofs, having a bridle of linked gold on his head, and upon him a saddle of costly gold. And in the youth's hand were two spears of silver...of an edge to wound the wind, and cause blood to flow...A gold-hilted sword was upon his thigh, the blade of which was of gold, bearing a cross of inlaid gold of the hue of the lightening of heaven...Before him were two brindled white-breasted greyhounds, having strong collars of rubies about their necks reaching from the shoulder to the ear. And the one that was on the left side bounded across to the right side, and the one on the right to the left, and like two sea-swallows sported around him...And the blade of grass bent not beneath him, so light was his courser's tread as he journeyed towards the gate of Arthur's Palace."

(The Mabinogion)

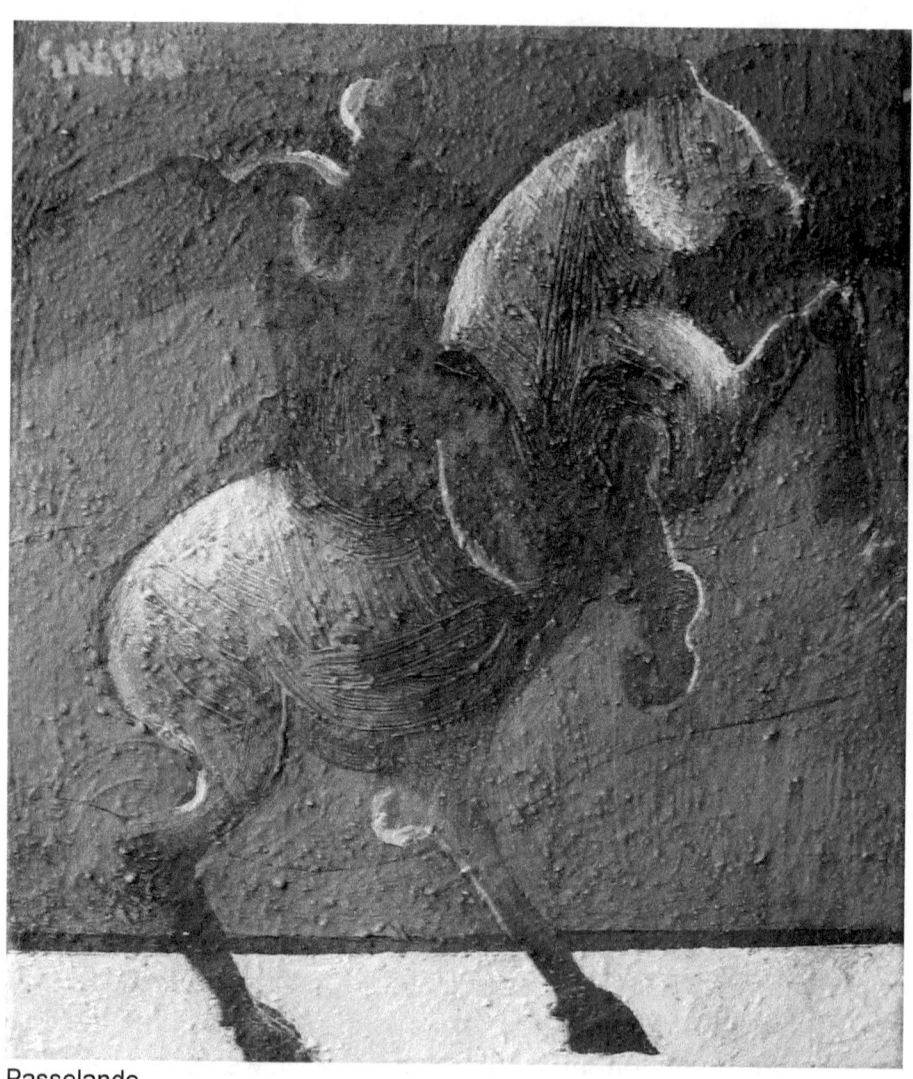

Passelande

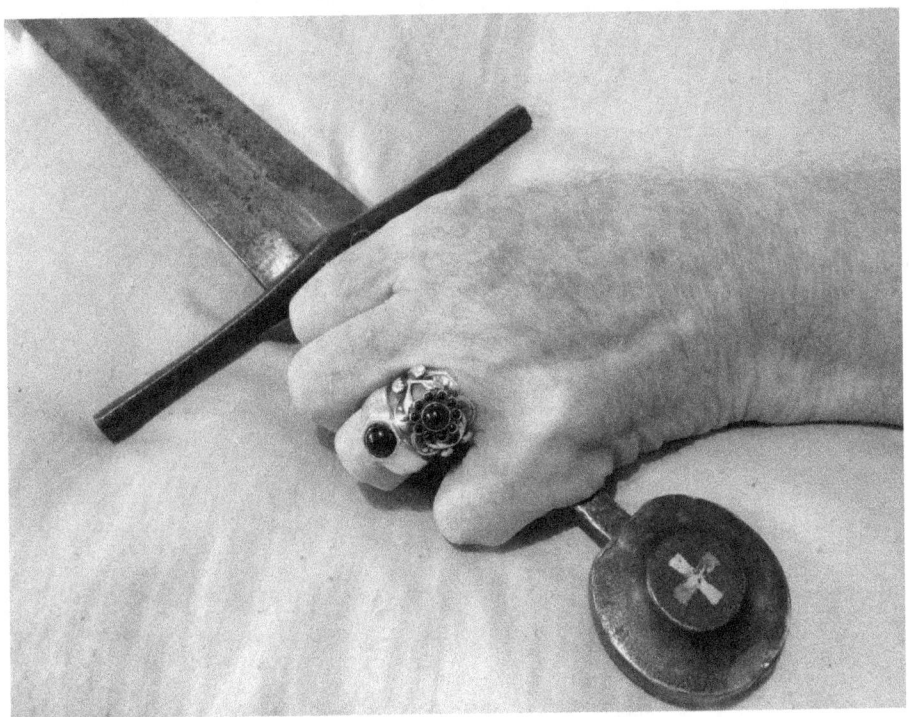

Geoffrey with sword and rings

The Painter

"Exposed by nature's natural eye
Visions excepted but unseen
Life's blindness is resighted
Reborn by the painter's dream"

Geoffrey Key

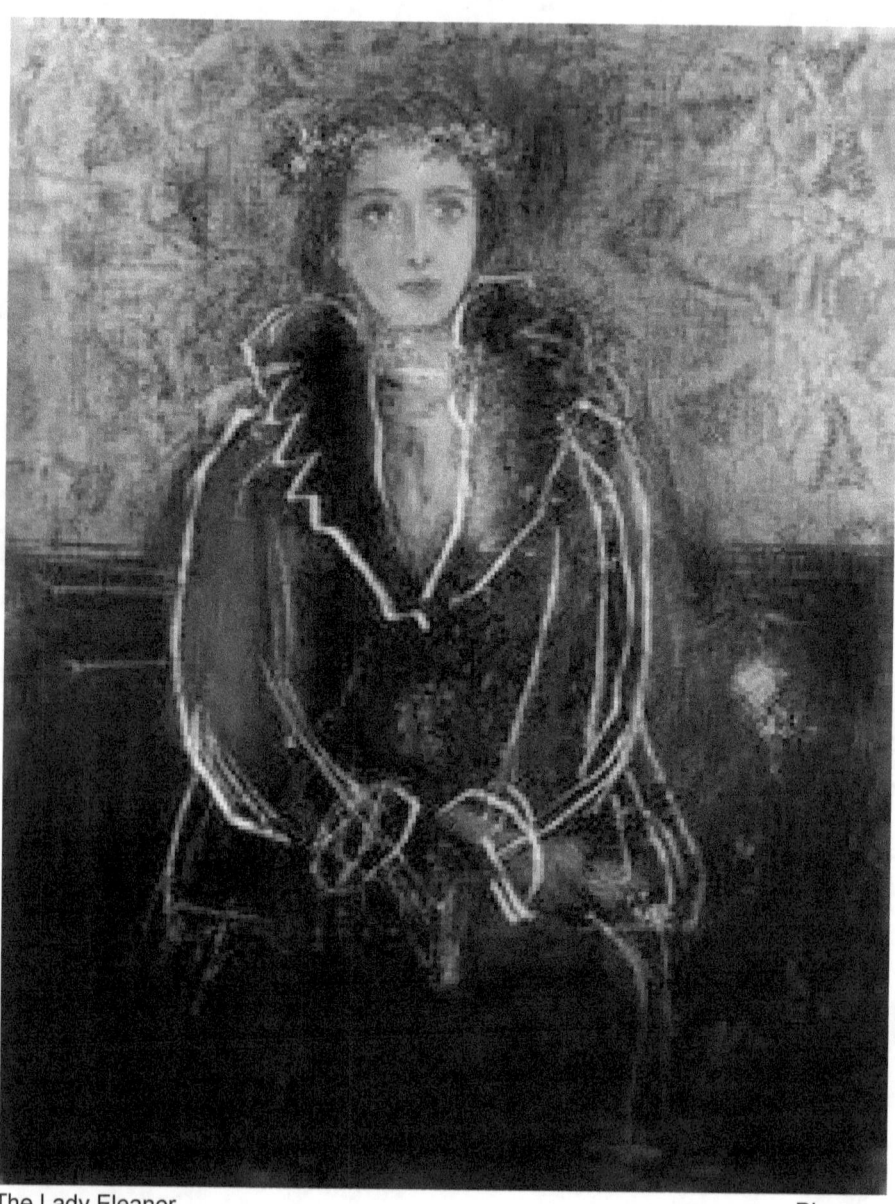

The Lady Eleanor — Picasso

Geoffrey the Fair and Eleanor of Epona

Some characters and stories – only the greatest ones, and only the ones which hold and compel human belief, can become the bases of universes in their own right. Real humans must be found to take the major roles, and to play them out. But eventually, like the Returning Rider you will be drawn back to your own time and place. The stage is set for drama and adventure, but the home universe is what we eventually return to.

Most of all in the world the grey-horse enjoyed his solitary rides with Eleanor. He had previously been with the Cestrecir Hundred, the proud leader guided by the Master of the hunt. At first he had felt nervous when hacking out alone, as he was so used to being with a large group of equines, but now he delighted in enjoying the countryside alone with Eleanor, because she always re-assured and inspired him by sharing her magical stories. The disappearing world of Fairy, and the White-Goddess was her domain. Her autumn musings were some of his favourites; he knew that her birthday was in October. "Spiders embroideries. Early on bright sunny mornings, before the dew had lifted, the night labours of spiders reveal schemes of sparkling threads over grass, crops and stubble in the fields. The horse shouldn't miss the opportunity to see this magical sight, and it should be pointed out whenever seen." Throughout their rides together she talked to him, and this made him feel that they were truly exploring and having unique adventures. In her complete empathy with horses she was a disciple of Xenophon, the ancient Greek master of horsemanship. Also, she believed in the interconnectedness of all living things.

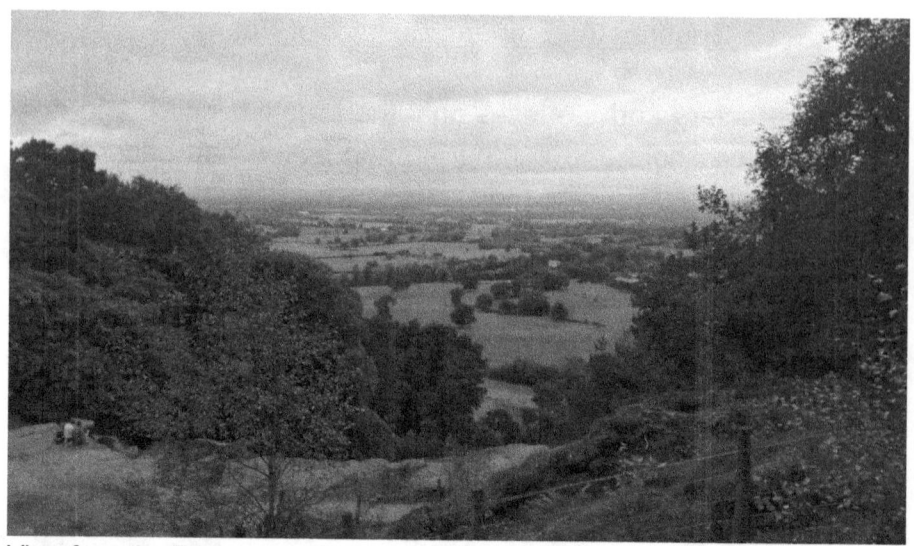

View from the Edge

When Eleanor was riding on her beautiful grey-horse she entered another world, just as her partner Geoffrey did when he was painting or creating sculptures in his studio high up on the third floor of the large house they shared. His work was based on memories of visions both past and present, and this use of a remembered or current vision distilled his images to a unique and creative whole. Although he had been born in Rusholme, and lived all his life in the north of England, he was an artist of international renown and disliked being identified as belonging to a narrow regional category termed 'Northern Art', which had taken Lowry as its spearhead. As one critic had pointed out, the only thing that Geoffrey and Lowry had in common was "this obsessive desire to paint what the artist has yet to find – something that is not there but should be." This quest for something as it might be rather than as it looks, united Eleanor and Geoffrey in their journey to traverse the paths between a possible labyrinth of worlds, and learn through their dreams. The horses in Geoffrey's paintings were those on which gods and heroes ride. Geoffrey and Eleanor were both acute observers and dreamers and felt that they were haunted by events past and present. Once on horseback, Eleanor resembled the White Spirit of Celtic mythology.

As Eleanor and Bluestone (which was the proper name of the grey-horse) were passing over the land on this misty autumn morning, they shared their musings as they both watched the brindled, white-breasted whippet, Nel, run ahead. On her strong leather collar were shining rubies, and as she bounded through the abundant damp leaves she resembled a sea-swallow darting and sporting in the air. Suddenly, Eleanor wondered if what she was seeing was really in front of her, or was some sort of vision taken from the Mabinogian, an old book of Welsh fairy stories and legends, which included tales of Arthur. Perhaps in her head she was re-writing those ancient myths with their magical ambience and otherworldly feel. When riding, Eleanor often felt that, like myth itself, she belonged both to vanished worlds and worlds still to come. This sense of battling her way through the dreams and patterns of myth was especially acute whenever she rode Bluestone on Alderley Edge. The place names were so evocative, Thieves Hold, Severn Firs, Goldenstone, Stormy-Point, and Saddlebole, to name but a few of the landmarks on the journey. Of course, Eleanor knew the legend in all its variations and had heard it recounted on many occasions, but most strange of all, she had more than once personally encountered a Merlin-like old man walking on the road beyond Peover. Eleanor knew that the story existed deep within the psyche of her own childhood.

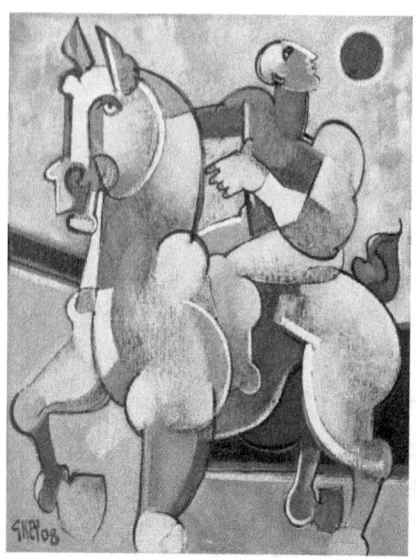
Rider with Red Sun

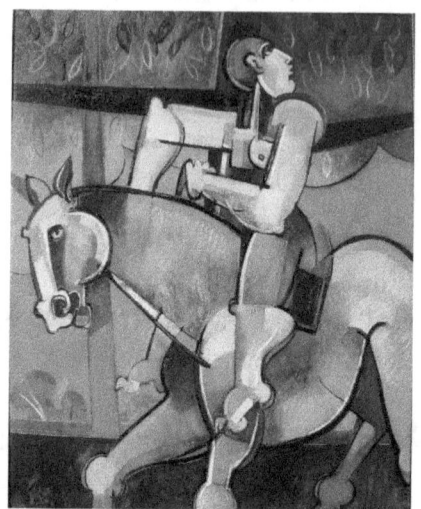
Rider in the Wood

According to a folk-tale, a farmer from Mobberley once had his horse purchased by a wizard for the use of a king and his knights who were slumbering beneath the Edge. In the cave One hundred and forty Knights in Silver chainmail armour, and a milk-white Steed beside all but one of the sleeping knights. The farmer had been on his way to Macclesfield Fair to sell his horse, but when he reached Alderley Edge the horse stopped and refused to move, no matter what the farmer did. He saw an old man standing by the side of the road, holding a staff in his hand. The old man offered to buy the horse, but the farmer refused, thinking that he would get a better price at the market. The farmer went on to Macclesfield, and although everybody praised the mare, nobody would buy her. So, at the end of the day, the farmer set off for home. When he arrived at Alderley Edge the old man was waiting for him. This time he did agree to sell, and the old man told the farmer to follow him. The farmer travelled down the long tunnel and left his horse in the cave, having been given golden jewels in payment for her. The Old Man said that the knights were waiting to fight the last battle of the world, and he had to wake them when that moment came. The one missing horse had now been found and would lie with his knight, in an enchanted sleep. When the iron-gate closed behind him and he found himself on the Edge, it was night and a full moon was shining. Never again could he find the entrance to the cave. Eleanor had reworked this legend many times in her head and shared it with Bluestone as they rode across Alderley, but she also knew that her horse was an inspiration, creating thoughts capable of carrying one to faraway times and places. Just as Geoffrey's studio Campion was a sacred 'poer place' where the supernatural became tangible, and boundaries between worlds were breached, so was Bluestone the hoof-proud Arthurian steed with Eleanor on his back, perhaps a messenger between the living and the dead.

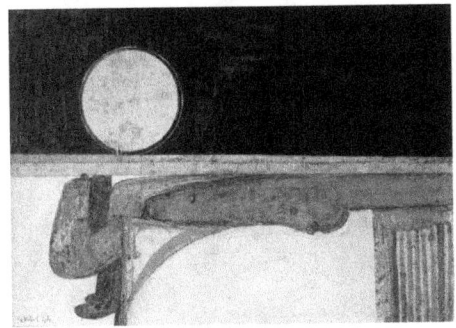

Nab Moon

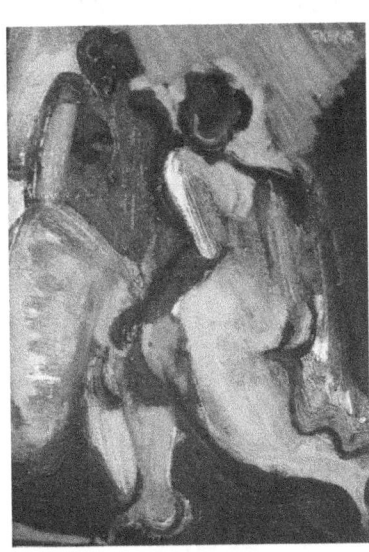

Nab Meeting

In the time of Merlin and King Arthur the horse was a symbol of shamanic journeys between this world and others. The horse enabled beings to travel to other worlds and learn through meditation and prophecy. The Anglo-Saxons called death 'faring forth', going on a journey from this world to the next, and winning eternal glory with the edges of their swords. Heroes and horses were one and the same. Eleanor thought of Geoffrey's early preoccupation with the Nab, a strange hill in Derbyshire, which he had obsessively painted for two years. Whiteley Nab was a primeval place associated over the century with Druids, Celts, and Saxons. In more recent decades it had been a site for Warlocks, Witches, and Wizards, all reputed to be endowed with dark magical powers. It was said that King Arthur had fought the Saxons there as nearby Glossop was one of the strongholds of the ancient Britons. Thus the Nab, which met alike the storms of winter and the glow of summer had long ago been the scene of conflict with the Saxon invader. For Geoffrey and Eleanor it remained a place mantled in mystery, but Geoffrey had found his place in the drama of the Nab, by painting it over and over again. At first his images had been abstract but gradually figures emerged. Omnipresent in his later images of horse and rider merging into one, are references to the Nab landscape in the presence of the moon. Eleanor felt that she and Geoffrey knew much about the unknown and unseen, testimony to which was their collection at home of antique Bellarmines, possibly used as witches-bottles many centuries ago. Eleanor whispered this poem of transformation to Bluestone.

> I must have been a cloud once
> Drifting and lonely
> A crosser of borders,
> White-bearded father of rains,

Caresser of soaring birds,
Painter of rainbows,
A lonely shadow over lonely plains

I must have gone once
Through somewhere else,
Over other ranges,
Other shades of green,
Where there are no friends
No strangers,
And no sounds carried by another wind.

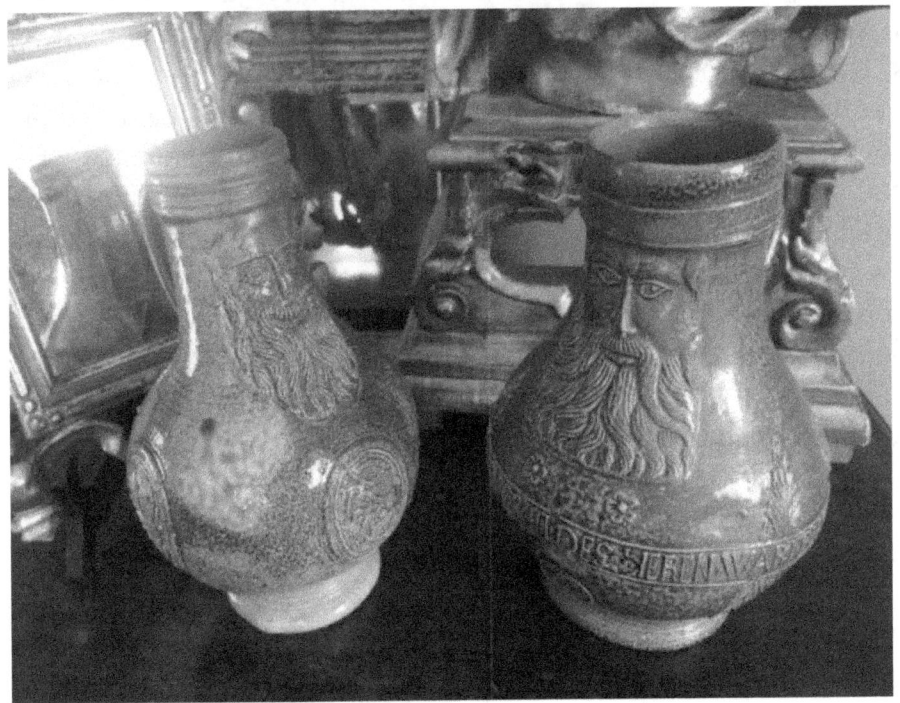
Bellarmines

Like the writer Camus, Eleanor believed that Autumn is a second spring when every leaf is a flower, and she delighted in this season. "When we rode out on our own I used to tell him stories about the knights sleeping at Alderley and how they were waiting for a grey-horse and how in Autumn the fairies had balls and parties and you could see all their gold and scarlet cloaks (leaves) thrown on the ground in the woods – and similar musings".

Certainly the Edge was a very special place, ancient, holy, and possessed, where it seemed that boundaries between worlds could be breached. In mediaeval times the horse was believed to have a liminal role, and its skull was credited with the ability to see things invisible to ordinary mortals. Iron-Age horse sacrifice in the wetlands, such as those she now gazed down upon, was to do with control of borders to the Underworld. Not far away was Lindow Common in which lay the black lake. Lindow man had been a first century AD victim of Druid ritual sacrifice. He had suffered the Celtic triple death. He was strangled, hit on the head, and his throat cut. And as Eleanor rode Bluestone across the high long-backed hill, her thoughts become increasingly eerie and sombre. She thought of Geoffrey's Nab painting in which human figures emerge from abstracted landscapes, in the presence of Orbs. The mesmeric iconography of Orbs had remained with Geoffrey throughout his life.

The sun was struggling to pierce the thick mists of an autumnal early morning, but cast a red glare over the surrounding vapours, which assumed a variety of strange forms. The scene reminded Eleanor of one of Geoffrey's oil paintings 'Horse with Red Sun', in which horse and rider were gilded by the life-giving fireball in the sky. The early Celts, Saxons, and Danes, identified the head of a horse as a symbol of power, vitality and the sun. And when Eleanor trotted past the Old Copper Mine workings, she thought of the story of the mighty sword Excalibur, pulled from the stone. The bronze-age mining activity on the Edge, the earliest in Britain, and the eerie caves once occupied by the miners, might have been the source of the legend. Alderley could have been the site of the forging of the first sword, by Merlin a metallurgist. At home in Salford, Geoffrey had a beautiful early mediaeval sword, circa 1300, the cross on the hilt in gilden latten. The words of an early Celtic warrior came to mind. "I need a sword because I am not a woman. A man unarmed is no man at all." The sword had come attached to a myth. It was said that a spirit lived within the sword hilt, and that this enchantment was a gift from the wizard Merlin, the first owner of the sword. Dreams and shadows and golden moon lay within the sword, and its power was greater by far than that of the famous Excalibur.

The story of the sleeping King and his similarly enchanted knights, who will awaken and rise again when the country is in dire need of a Saviour, is claimed by at least three different locations including Cornwall, Wales, and Cheshire. The tale of the Enchanter of Alderley Edge had first appeared in print in 1805, although the story itself dated back to 1753. And later on a servant girl named Ellen Beck claimed to have seen the wizard's iron gates up on the Edge. Her subsequent suicide after betrayal by her lover, led to the story of her ghost haunting the Edge as the woman in white. Young children playing on the Edge have recounted stories of hearing music and the sounds of whinnying horses coming from within the ground. It is well known that children feel close to the eternal because when you are a small child everything seems eternal, including love. The greatest artists share the honest vision of the child.

Eleanor was telling Bluestone the story of the farmer on horseback who had met Merlin, when she saw an odd looking old man: "A man on the road – I'd only just taken responsibility for Bluestone when this really happened on the road heading to Peover Hall. A very, very elderly chap, dressed in traditional battered tweeds, wax jacket, cap and wellies was walking along towards us – all alone, no dog, no mud spattered quad bike, just walking. We just exchanged the usual 'good morning' when he said very pointedly 'that 'oss – that one – it'll do you no harm'. I assumed he was someone from the Celestrecir Hundred where Bluestone had been the Master's horse but no-one recognised his description..." Eleanor wondered if the horse-skull, which she kept in her office at home was enabling her to see and hear things invisible and inaudible to others.

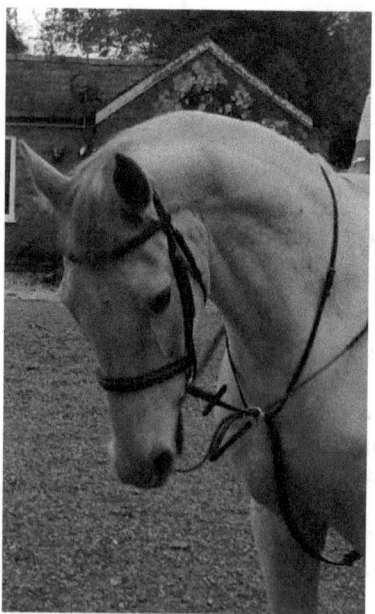

Eleanor's horse Bluestone

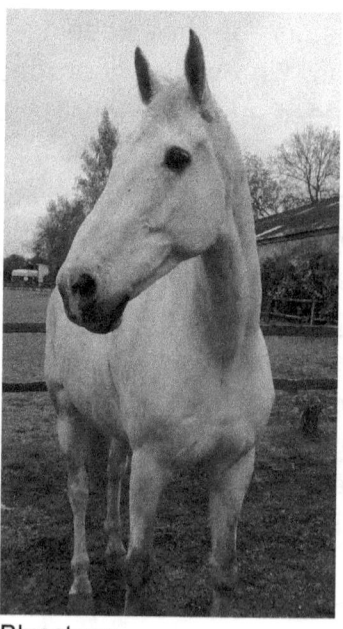

Bluestone

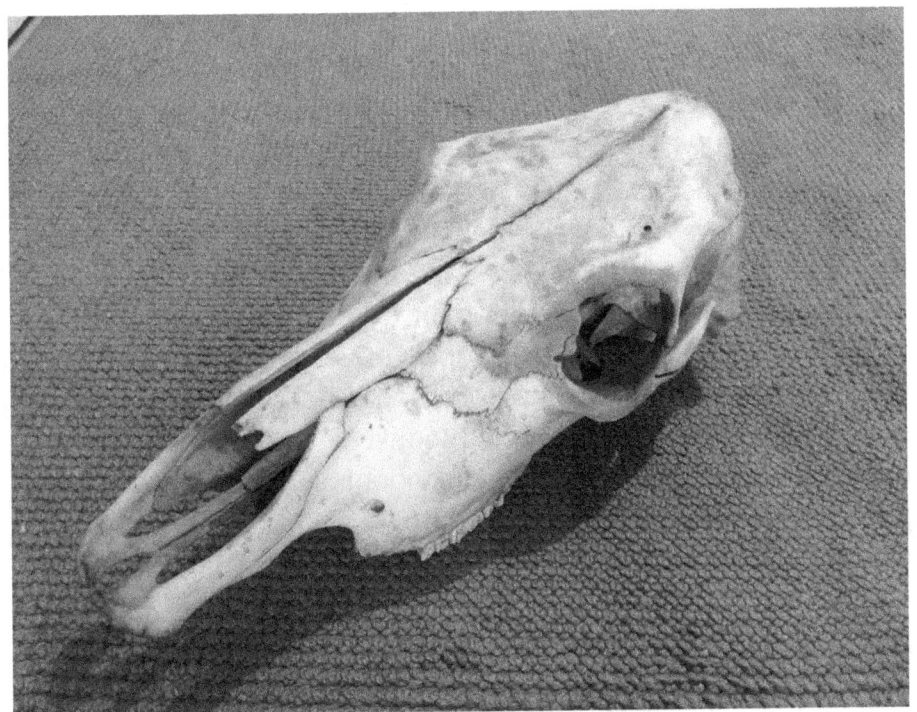
Skull of a horse

In retelling the legend of Alderley Edge to her horse Bluestone when they rode out alone, had she invited an encounter with Merlin? It was said that the famous magician always kept a magical skull close by, and that his wand was made from a branch of the sacred and protective alder tree. "Here in this place, we are beyond the reach of time." Eleanor told her horse stories about the knights sleeping at Alderley and how they were waiting for a grey horse – and how in Autumn the fairies had balls and parties and you could see all their gold and scarlet cloaks (leaves) thrown on the ground in the woods... Having passed the old man on the road, Eleanor's mind turned to the wonderful power and beauty of Geoffrey's depictions of horses in oils, sculpture and drawings. Although his relationship with horses was solely aesthetic, his observations of the ways in which horse and rider became as one – showing harmony co-operation and trust were down to his keen eye and perception, especially of Eleanor riding. Proximity to the real thing was not something he relished, and he had never ridden – but his artistic portraits of horses and their riders were made in heaven, and were visionary. Her thoughts returned to his early obsession with the Nab, a strange bleak hill in Derbyshire which had been his sole subject for two years. Painting the hill for two years had developed his unique style and freed him form earlier influences. Those strange semi-abstracted often moonlit figures and horses had expressed an otherworldly and fluid identity, which had entranced her. When Eleanor entered Geoffrey's studio, a poetic, creative space all his own, she felt that they were both beyond the reach of time and had escaped the prosaic. It was a world of beauty, joy, wonder and enchantment, with an inevitable element of fear and melancholy synonymous with the visionary. As his companion, lover, and muse she felt this deeply, especially in the arm-embrasure portraits with birds or flowers. His portraits of birds often in association with human figures, evoked the spirit of Classical mythology and power in repose. As the angels of the earth they seemed to occupy a dwelling-place that very much appealed to the sensibilities of Geoffrey the artist and Seamus Heaney the poet. "I like the in-betweenness of up and down, of being on the earth and of the heaven…between the dream world and the given world, because you don't just want photography and you don't want fantasy". When the strong and powerful Geoffrey placed his ring-adorned hands on hers, those rings seemed magical, like the runic rings of the Saxon Kings and Warriors. Eleanor felt that these mysterious and beautiful rings transmitted power and healing. It was said that they would staunch bleeding from man or horse and would also heal a wounded soul. In the Studio was the defining window's square of sky;

> "Her face receives the sun
> And softens it. Angled by
> Her arm's embrasure,
> White architectural distances
> Ride sleeping in the clear truce of her eye"

Eleanor's bible in training and riding horses was Xenophon. It was he of the Greek bronze age who had written that the horses of gods and heroes are always in the act of rearing up, and that there was no finer sight than a line of horses in a regiment of cavalry, prancing and snorting all together. Geoffrey's riders were informed by his knowledge of ancient sculptures and reliefs, alternately appearing to charge out of the canvas or freeze in attitude. There was tremendous classical power, and energy of line, form and colour.

Just as Eleanor was sharing her further musings with Bluestone something startled him and he reared up and snorted, not in alarm but in glory. Eleanor's Alderley Legend and encounter with the Enchanter was about to begin in the past.

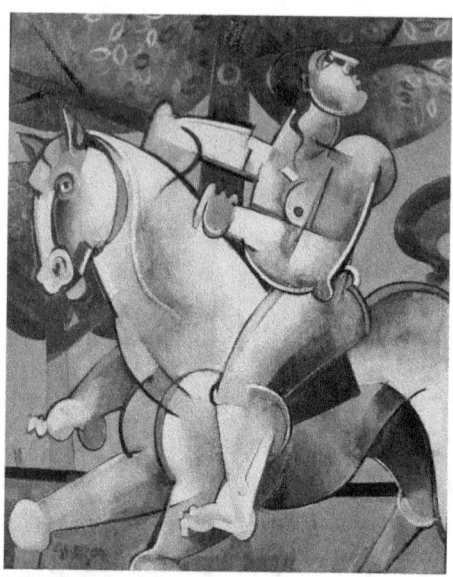
Woodland Rider

In the time before King Arthur, Britain was like a great mountain or oak tree that had been cut down and shattered into fragments by a giant axe. The country needed to be brought together and united under a great leader; otherwise it would be conquered and destroyed by the repeated incursions and invasions by tribes from Saxony. Now that the Romans had departed to protect their own conquests in Germania, the people of Britain were feeling very vulnerable to attack. Britain urgently needed knights to win eternal glory with the edges of their swords. Horses and their heroic riders were longed for.

Unfortunately, the Romano-British had invited the Saxons to fight the Celts on their behalf, so when the romans withdrew, they left the Anglo-Saxons dominating lowland Britain, and they were fighting the indigenous Britons. Attend to this story and you will learn of great heroes and their adventures for the glory of the Round Table. Red blood will run freely and many knights fall to their deaths before Arthur, the wisest, worthiest, and most noble warrior is recognised as the great and rightful King of Britain - "The Once and Future King".

When the son of King Uther Pendragon was born he was entrusted to the care of Merlin the magical wizard. Uther had fought many battles against the Saxons, but he also had many enemies within Britain, who were trying to steal his lands.

Merlin who had the ability to change into a bird took the baby boy to Sir Ector who promised to care for him, protect him and not reveal the secret of his birth.

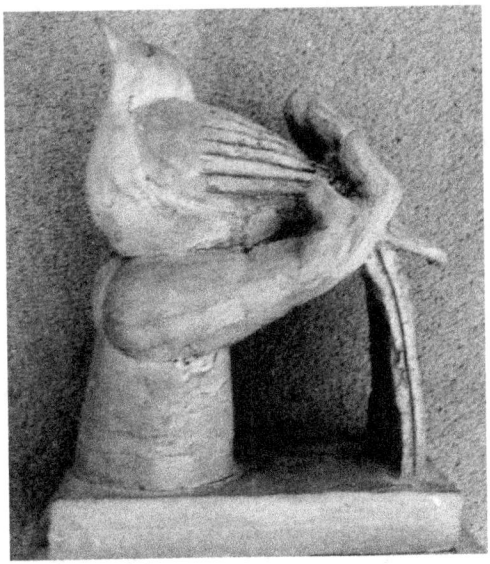

Bird in Hand

When Arthur was about sixteen, Sir Ector arranged a magnificent tournament to test the strength of all his knights, and his young son Sir Kay. Arthur was Kay's Squire, looking after his weapons and armour. Unfortunately, Arthur had forgotten to pack Kay's sword, so a very angry Sir Kay sent Arthur back to fetch another sword.

Arthur remembered that on the way to the tournament he had seen a sword sticking out of a rock in a nearby churchyard, so he ran to fetch it. When Arthur grabbed the handle of the great sword and pulled very hard, it slid easily from the stone.

He hurried back to the tournament but just before he could give the sword to his foster brother, Kay's father intervened. "Where, Arthur, did you find that sword?" he asked. "I found it sticking out of a rock in the churchyard" replied Arthur.

Sir Ector then called together all the knights taking part in the tournament and ordered them to return to the churchyard. He placed the sword back into the stone, but none of the knights could pull it free! Young Arthur was the only one who could pull the sword form the stone, and this meant that Arthur was the rightful King of Britain! Sir Ector explained that the magical wizard Merlin had protected the boy form harm by keeping secret his true identity.

Although Arthur felt unsure of himself and did not really know how to be a King, Merlin promised to help and protect him in every way, saying "do not be afraid. Once everyone sees your swordsmanship and horsemanship, they will follow you. To help you train as a great equestrian we have the Lady Eleanor to assist you. She will teach you to ride like a god and defeat the Saxons. Under her guidance you will become a great and fearless warrior, leading your brave knights into battle".

The Arthurian Lady Eleanor

The sole Lady to be given the honour of a seat at King Arthur's famous Round Table was Lady Eleanor of Epona, named for the Roman and Celtic goddess of horses. She was a woman of great beauty, mystery and magic, black-haired and green-eyed. Although not herself a warrior knight, she trained and cared for all the riding and War-Horses in the Royal Stable. As the only woman at Arthur's Round Table, Eleanor felt rather like the Queen in a game of chess – the powerful piece on the board in what was a mediaeval history lesson in miniature. Under her guidance Arthur's mounted warriors were now set on the dark plain like gigantic chessmen, certain to defeat the Saxon foot-soldiers. Some said that Eleanor had first come from Celtic Wales or Rome, or Gaul, but none really knew. She was celebrated for her incomparable skill in horsemanship, and many mounted soldiers who adored her thought that Eleanor had always existed, probably since the beginning of time. They could not imagine a world without Eleanor; they worshiped her as a goddess. Her devoted followers believed that she had trained Xanthos, Balios and Pedasos, the three horses of Achilles, whose immortal nature was deeply upset by the death of mortal Patroclus. For him they wept. Just like Eleanor, they had been caught up in the majesty and misery of man.

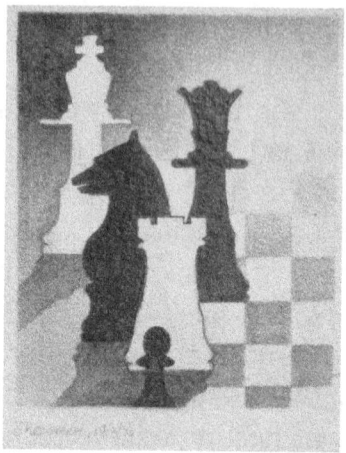

Trevor Grimshaw Chessmen

It was the Lady Eleanor who had first had the idea of defeating the invading Saxon enemies of Arthur by using the cavalry in battle, as other cultures like that of Xenophon had done in the ancient past.

Kind Eleanor also had the unique gift of being able to talk to horses, especially King Arthur's favourite horse the great Passelande, dauntless and eternal. He was the most gallant of Arthur's noble horses, a joy and terror to behold, and one on which only gods and heroes could ride into battle.

Eleanor's great prowess and empathy with horses enabled the valiant Knights of The Round Table to defeat their barbarian enemy of foot-soldiers, even though they were vastly outnumbered. Her greatest triumph was to be the battle of Badon Hill at which the Saxons were routed.

One of her greatest challenges at present was the equestrian education of a Saxon nobleman and mercenary, who having fought valiantly against the Roman invasion of Saxony, had now decided to fight with the Britons. As a young boy, he had been sent to Rome and forced to join the army, so he knew something of horses, but he had later defected to the Saxon foot-soldiers. Geoffrey the Fair goldenes Haar Seaxneat Hringwear was indeed a most handsome Lord of the sword. His sword was said to be enchanted and of far greater force than that of Arthur's. It was Geoffrey and Eleanor who were the real saviours of Celtic Britain and the ancient pagan magic of the Whitethorn Wood. Having formerly been a member of the Saxon Infantry, he wore the flamboyant Landsknecht uniform of brightly coloured cut-trousers, jerkin, and feathered hat. His Saxon symbols of great manliness were his beard and long flowing curly hair. He was given a further epithet and title by those who were fortunate enough to know him well – gesceppend – the great minded one, deep and complex. In his days as a Saxon warrior, Geoffrey carried the flag with the emblem of the Sahson, the black steed, which expressed his longing to fight on horseback and lead the cavalry rather than the foot-soldiers.

Under the influence and guidance of the Lady Eleanor he would change from a renowned Saxon mercenary foot-soldier to a glorious mounted warrior of world renown – a windelocces Ridwiga, leading an Eored, a mountain troop. Geoffrey remembered his men being mocked by the Romans for their inability to ride. The Saxons originally used horses only for transport and strategic purposes. Centuries later, when the Anglo-Saxons vanquished the Britons, they had themselves become mounted warriors and their graves contain the skeletons of horses, accorded the same heroic status as their riders.

But in Arthur's time the Britons fought on horseback against an army of Saxon Foot-soldiers, whom they defeated around 500AD when Arthur's army was at its most successful and famous. The mythological Arthur of all Regions is remembered as a mounted knight and his men fought as cavalrymen. It would be many hundreds of years before the invading Saxons learned from the Britons how to become mounted warriors like the Germanic Warlords Hengist (Stallion) and Horsa (horse). For the time being the invading Saxons were barbarians, Teutonic fighters with neither armour nor cavalry.

Now that his Court was fully assembled, and Eleanor was the chief advisor to all his brave knights, Arthur decided that the time had come to destroy the invading Saxons. During this long war Arthur broke the sword that he had pulled from the enchanted stone, but Merlin the wizard knew exactly where to find a replacement. He guided Arthur through a dark, misty wood until they reached a ghostly lake. When Arthur looked at the lake he saw a magnificent sword rise out of the water. The sword was held by the Lady of the Lake, and Arthur took the sword, which was called Excalibur, from her outstretched hand. Merlin explained that the sword had been forged on the mystical Isle of Avalon, and that its magic along with the cream of the cavalry on iron-grey horses, and the healing power of the Well-Head waters, would enable Arthur to defeat the barbaric foot-soldiers from alien land. Geoffrey would be at the head of the mounted knights, and lead them into battle. He would fight in twelve bloody battles, and his greatest victory would be at Badon Hill. And when the days of the fellowship were over, and Mordred punished for his treachery, Arthur and Excalibur would return to the misty Isle of Avalon.

Accompanied by her devoted whippet Guinelot, the Lady Eleanor loved to exercise the horses by riding across the miles of farmland, open moor, and dense forest that made up Britain in all its beauty and enchantment. Whilst riding out she would tell them stories of Goblins and Fairies, which although occasionally frightening, would always conclude with a message of reassurance to calm the horses.

"I've mentioned the autumn parties and the golden cloaks thrown on the ground, these started as the Solstice approached. In the woods Fairies can get very noisy, even to human ears, especially in rain or wind. To horses the noise is much greater and they can hear the higher pitched squealing and laughing that we can't, plus they can understand fairy language which can be quite shocking to a noble horse. These histrionics are never unkind, though, and any really outrageous carryings on can be subdued if you always remember, when crossing the bridge crossing the fairies' brook, to greet them politely.

In another part is the Goblins' bridge. This crosses a murky brown stream, such as Goblins prefer for its bad smell and general unpleasantness. Goblins are very, very, ill- mannered. They think nothing of hiding in bushes and behind trees and as a horse approaches shouting out cruel and disrespectful remarks; shaking the leaves and branches and performing in any way they can think to cause alarm. Humans cannot see or hear Goblins so are often surprised when their horse spooks at seemingly nothing. Some riders blame the horse for misbehaving, instead of being a steadying guide, and this causes Goblins to roll about with laughter, often making matters worse. So on approaching the Goblin's bridge - a firm, confident - 'we know you're there and we won't fall for your nonsense' is reassuring all round."

All the knights' horses listened to Eleanor and when they had to face the horror and carnage of battle they remembered her magical stories and kind caressing hands as they galloped to war. If they were mortally wounded their final thoughts would be of her and the stories she told them when out riding, which they had so loved in the past. They hoped to meet her again in the blessed afterlife at Avalon, as like myth itself she belonged both to vanished worlds and worlds still to come – Like the glorious Passelande " I pass but shall not die". When a great British warrior died a statue of Eleanor was always placed on his grave to bless him on his journey to Avalon.

Much of Eleanor's time was now taken up in helping Geoffrey to overcome his wariness around unpredictable horses, and to encourage him to relax in their company. He loved their beauty and power, which resembled his own, but was reluctant to get too close, take the reins and mount. Eleanor explained to the warrior with flowing golden curls and penetrating, all-seeing eyes that horses respond to voices and enjoy being spoken to as equals, as well as being caressed. Her 'Grey-Horse Musings' were a beautiful example of how to interact with and reassure a horse. Tell your beloved companion a story and he will feel happy and relaxed:

"The Grey Horse

This is a tale set long, long ago, about a man named Elric. It is also about his horse, which needs no name.

the whistling wood

Some people call them fallen leaves, while others say that in late autumn, woodland fairies cast aside the golden cloaks they wore for the Samhain revels. These revels are huge parties, which take place every year on 31 October, when the natural year ends, harvest is complete and as the dark, quiet time begins.

It was now mid-November and in the early dawn light Elric walked his grey horse through the rustling remnants of the fairy cloaks that lay on the ground in Whistling Wood. This ancient, mixed woodland with its venerable, gnarled, trees bordered Elric's farm on the North side. Its pathways provided the shortest yet most interesting route to the market town some five miles away.

up the hill

At the edge of the wood the pathway widened, dark ancient trees giving way to the lighter tones of silver birch, stark against the golden carpet underfoot. Elric and the grey horse began the long climb uphill. As they neared the cliff edge that formed the highest point for miles around, the layering light was soon to herald the spectacular rising of a huge red sun. It seemed the day was to be special. The hill, locally called the Edge, was known for legend and magic. It stood over the farms and villages of the plain below, a constant presence. Beneath its slopes lay labyrinths of caves first formed by nature and later worked by forebears from long ago.

the reason for the journey

But Elric's thoughts were weighed down with worries. For a second year, his farm and those of all his neighbours had suffered poor harvests. Spring and Summer weather had not been kind, the harvest festivals had been sad affairs which only fairies and their friends had really enjoyed. Barns that should have been filled to the rafters stood almost empty and winter had yet to begin. For Elric, his only choice was to go to market and seek to buy in feed from elsewhere. For this he needed money, which he did not have, or something to sell or exchange.

The grey horse was all he had of value. Elric was sad to have to think of selling his workmate and friend, but the hardships he and his other farm animals (the grey horse included, were he to stay) would face left no choice.

So it was with heavy steps Elric trudged onwards, not noticing the hubbub of wild creatures as he passed. Rabbits bobbed and scuttled, a fox slunk under the hedgerow, myriad birds darted and swooped, yet Elric was oblivious, lost in fearful thought.

the warning

The reverie was soon broken. As they neared the Edge, the Grey Horse was startled; he raised his head, twitching his ears, every sinew in his body poised for flight. Elric spoke soothingly; as yet he could see nothing unusual. But within moments a strange figure came into view. Slowly, a seemingly aged, bent, figure, with long grey hair and clothed as if he had been outdoors for weeks, came towards them. He nodded a greeting and fixed Elric with the gaze of his pale blue gimlet eyes.

After an uncomfortably long silence, the man spoke.

'You'll be planning to sell the horse today.' His tone gave the words the quality of a statement rather than a question. 'Maybe', said Elric. 'You won't', the man replied, his tone this time tinged with sympathy. 'But I wish you well'. And so they parted, Elric feeling disconcerted, and not a little puzzled as to who the man was, why he had approached him and how he knew his business. (The latter might have been the easiest to guess.)

onwards to the market

The road into town was busy with carts, barrows, people and animals on foot, hoof and trotter. The atmosphere was hopeful; despite the general worries there was always the possibility of fortune striking and a good deal being struck. It was a day for seeing friends and neighbours, of catching up with news, good and bad. But not many people had good news.

Market day was usually alive with excitement, but today far more people were hoping to sell than to buy. Some managed to barter and swap, but there was little good business. No one could offer Elric anything like the proper value of the Grey Horse. Even the food and drink stalls had a bad day.

back to the Edge

Elric headed back towards home. He had started out with a feeling of sad acceptance, but now he just felt despair. He had nothing to show for a long walk. At least the Grey Horse had eaten along the way, but Elric was hungry. They slowly retraced their steps as the light began to fade and an evening mist started to fall. As they left the road from the town and started along the path the landscape felt increasingly eerie. Bats began their twilight flights, from the distance the mournful evening cry of a dogfox could be heard. It was the sort of time when no one would have been surprised if goblins and boggarts were on the prowl.

As if from nowhere, a figure appeared, just as the bent old man had done that morning. His face looked the same, weather-beaten with piercing blue eyes, yet the long grey matted hair was now white and swept back as if finely brushed. The hunched, cowed form of earlier was now proud, upright and tall; he possessed an air of authority.

'So, my friend, you still have the Grey Horse.' This needed no answer, since it was clearly a statement rather than a question. But Elric recognised a gentleness in his tone and welcomed being addressed as 'my friend'. Tired and hungry, a friend was what he needed.

The man went on: 'I know what brought you this way, I know the troubles in the land and I could help you find a solution. It will take courage and trust. First, I ask that you come with me.'

the cave

Elric felt disconcerted, but at that moment thought he may as well follow, at least for now, and so long as wherever he was being taken was not too far.

So meekly he shrugged and the three set off down a steeply descending path, the man leading. The way was just beginning to get rather too muddy and slippery for the Grey Horse to manage when the man led them, by a sudden left turn, into a gaping cavern. This appeared to be a natural cave in the sandstone cliff. Inside the ground was soft and dry. The cave stretched back into the cliff, and once well inside, where the roof space reached far overhead, Elric could see and feel the welcoming light and warmth of a blazing fire. The man bade Elric lead the horse to a water trough fed by an underground spring at the side of the cave. Nearby was a generous pile of sweet hay and a straw bed. The Grey Horse needed no tether to keep him there and he soon settled to munching the unexpected feast.

Meanwhile, seated by the fire, Elric too settled to share food and drink with his host. 'How should I address you?' Elric asked, conscious that he had no idea in whose company he found himself. 'You can choose, but some call me Emrys, others say Ambrose, there are other names too. For preference, well, I don't really mind. I think too much is read into names, like appearances. Were you surprised that I looked different when we met for the second time today?' Elric was secretly fairly bewildered, but decided to keep things simple. 'Yes, I was, but who am I to say how anyone should decide to look - and as to addressing you, I'm glad to have something to call you and I think I like Ambrose,' said Elric.

'And your horse,' said Ambrose, 'has he a name?' 'That is a mystery,' replied Elric. 'He probably does, but it is a secret that I have not been told.'

Ambrose was pleased to learn this. It suggested a private matter might soon be concluded, and his belief that Elric's troubles and those of others affected by the poor harvests would be simultaneously resolved.

Their meal concluded, Elric thanked Ambrose profusely, and apologised that he could not, for the present at least, repay the generosity. 'I know that,' said Ambrose. 'But I want to talk to you, and I could not do that while you were cold and hungry.' 'Now I want to show you something, and I want you to keep an open mind. We will need to walk a little way further into the caves.' Elric felt both obliged and intrigued. Also, Ambrose had been quite charming, almost charismatic and there seemed nothing really to fear.

They left the Grey Horse peacefully settled and ventured onwards. Ambrose carried a flaming torch he had lit from the fire - it cast a sufficient glow for them to see their immediate surroundings, but little further. They entered a long passage, narrowly bounded by sandstone walls, but thankfully high overhead and dry underfoot. At the end of the passage was a heavy iron-bound oak door.

the Guardians

Ambrose had the key, and paused before opening the door. He turned to Elric and said: 'Elric, you have a choice here. There is something behind this door, but you are not obliged to go through. We can turn back, you can leave with the Grey Horse and we shan't meet again. Or I'll take you through, but if I do, you'll have to make a promise first. That is to listen carefully to what I will tell you, which will be completely truthful, and to trust me. I want you to take a risk, to act without expectation of any reward. I want you to trust your own instincts regarding what is right and to decide accordingly.'

He gave Elric a few moments to think, but Elric broke the silence and said: 'let's go. Open the door'.

Beyond, the vista was not at all what Elric might have expected. Instead of another configuration of caves, this was something spectacular. Open to the skies, an archway led to a neatly laid courtyard garden surrounded by yellow stone buildings, illuminated by similar torches to that which Ambrose had brought from the cave. Simple but elegantly structured, one side was devoted to stables with hay loft and other offices above, another housed an indoor exercise school for the horses, while the remaining two sides provided dwelling places.

'Who lives here?' whispered Elric to Ambrose. He replied: 'It would take a long time properly to explain and I hope one day I'll be able to tell you more, but we generally see them as Guardians. They..., well, let's just say, they work to keep things in balance so that life can carry on.' That seemed rather an immense undertaking and Elric would have liked to ask how they so, but felt that now wasn't quite the right time. He wanted to know what Ambrose wanted him to do.

Ambrose anticipated Elric's reaction and said: 'There is a lot you could find out about the things they do, but for now, you can actually help, and what is in your power could make a very big difference. I have to ask you to do something as a pure act of generosity, without expecting anything in return. It would be a matter of pure trust.'

the question

Ambrose went on: 'I have known of you and your Grey Horse for a while. No matter how, but there is something special about you both. Especially, at this stage, the Grey Horse.' As he had promised, Elric listened. 'He isn't unique, there are many like him, but most are in partnership with those we call Guardians, like the occupants here. Look at the stables - there aren't any better appointed in the land, or the world. The horses have the best of care. Oh, and one other thing, once they find their own Guardian, they become immortal, like the Guardians.'

Seeing that one stable was vacant, Elric could sense what was coming next. 'You want me to give you the Grey Horse, don't you?' He took a deep breath and quickly continued: 'Don't say anything - I can't begin to understand what this is all about, I'm probably dreaming, but you have been kind and something tells me I should trust to fate. Take him, but take care of him. That's all I ask. I'll leave with just that assurance and be content. '

'You have taken a great and brave decision', Ambrose said. 'Let us give you shelter tonight.' But Elric declined. As attractive as the place of the Guardians was, having made his decision, he wanted to leave without delay. He had no idea what the future might hold, all he had left was an indistinct feeling of hope. Ambrose understood. 'I'll make arrangements so you need not walk.'

Return

Elric remembered little of the journey home. In the weeks to come, dreamlike recollections would come into his mind: a sense of riding the fleetest horse he had ever experienced, the company of ghostly riders, experiences of far-reaching visions reaching towards the dawn horizon.

Meanwhile, as he neared home, an astonishing, yet real, vision greeted him. The first views of his farm and those of his neighbours revealed barns and feed stores that were full to the point of abundance. Winter crops, previously stunted and delayed by the wet ground, were now growing as they should for the season. The sense and spirit all around was one of looking forward - the earlier dismal harvests a bad dream.

Once in sight of home, Elric found himself once more on foot. Although thrilled and bewildered by the sights he had just experienced, he walked on with some trepidation, steeling himself in anticipation for the dreadful feeling of loss, to the yard where once the Grey Horse had been stabled. Here he was to find the greatest mystery. Nearing the entrance, Elric was startled by a familiar whicker of greeting. A grey head appeared over the stable door. There was no explanation, just a golden streak of plaited hair in the Grey Horse's mane, to which was attached a disc of copper, bearing a runic inscription which Elric was later to discover meant 'guardian'.

And so, safe in the knowledge that winter was provided for, and in partnership with what he now knew to be the magical Grey Horse, Elric began to consider how he might play his part in keeping life in balance in the seasons to come. He had much to consider.

Next Chapters

Elric meets the green man

Winter Solstice
In which the earth begins to stir, new growth begins below ground
Red winter sun"

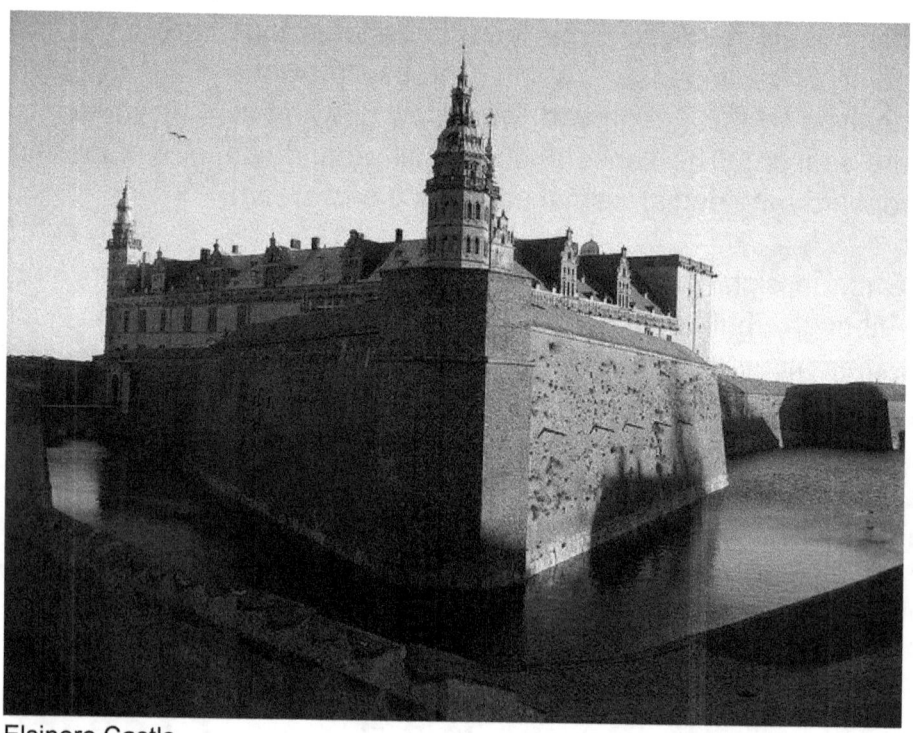

Elsinore Castle

Geoffrey's hands were adorned with beautiful, fascinating rings, which added to his magnetism and all powerful presence – "the joy of all beholders!" Geoffrey's Saxon culture had been based almost solely on war, and his King had to be a generous "Ring Giver". Fighting was a way of life, and blood-feuds were perpetual. The Germanic tribes hated peace and war was perceived as the only honourable code. The Ring-Giver was the King and he gave the rings, some inscribed with runes, to his greatest warriors. Some of the rings were set with stones and were a charm to stem bleeding. They had been made by the Danes and taken in wars against them, but Geoffrey the Saxon had secretly met Prince Hamlet of Denmark at Elsinore. There are beings in the Universe greater than men and lower than angels, who are known only in story and legend. These extraordinary beings know the doors between heaven and earth and have the power to open these doors of perception. In the future the Saxons and the Danes would become enemies, but at this time Geoffrey Wringwear was the trusted and beloved warrior friend of Hamlet. In any Universe there is nothing more powerful than a story, except perhaps for god himself. Prince Hamlet's castle defined itself like a living thing, like an embryo or work of art. Hamlet and Geoffrey knew the ways between the worlds, and were thus able to speak to the Ghosts.

Long ago the Danes had sometimes raided Britain along with Saxons, and the combined forces of Danish and Saxon warriors had met the Britons in battle. Also, there was another connection between Hamlet and Geoffrey. Hamlet's father's mother had been a Briton, so Hamlet felt sympathy for his friend, who was now fighting for the Britons against the Saxons and Danes. Most importantly of all, Geoffrey had seen and heard the ghost, who had prophesied Mordred's betrayal of Arthur and the fatal wounding of the rightful king, thus he was a witness to a terrifying spectre who demanded the swearing of a fatal oath. The melancholy prince gave Geoffrey a beautiful ring of silver and solemn black agate, which he would forever treasure along with the memory of Hamlet's words to him on seeing Yorick's skull:

"Heraldic Stance
Night plumed in velvet black"

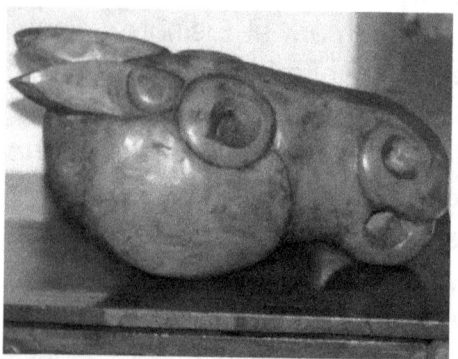

Horsehead

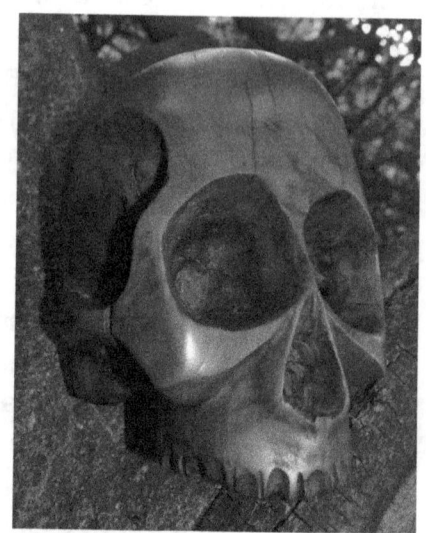

Yorick's skull

Xenophon had taught mankind the proper way to train and care for horses, and to make both man and horse successful in battle. He was Eleanor's inspiration and training manual for Geoffrey, as by the flowers of the fields he swore his oath to fight for King Arthur and the glory of the Round Table.

Xenophon had taught that riding is a partnership and it is the task of the rider to reassure the horse. "For what the horse does under compulsion…is done without understanding; and there is no beauty in it either, any more than if one should whip and spur a dancer…he should show off all his finest and most brilliant performances willingly and at a mere sign". If a man follows Xenophon's advice in caring for and training horses for war, then nothing except the inter-position of some divinity can prevent him becoming famous in the art of horsemanship.

Eleanor was identified with the Celtic Epona, goddess of horses, whereas although Geoffrey the Saxon had been a hostage in Rome and in the army as a youth, he had served as an infantryman. However, he saw at once the potential of well trained horses and longed to lead his fellow knights into bloody battle, riding his quick-footed horse, armoured like himself. He had been born in the sacred month of May, and was imbued with the male energy and virility of White Hawthorn Tree, in flower at his birth. Many would shed their blood and fall to their death in the wake of Geoffrey's hoof-beats, but Arthur would be seated on his throne with jewelled diadem and golden robe, and ruby-red goblets.

Arthur's Royal Riders would defeat the Saxon invaders, and whilst the King was engaged in battle both at home and across the sea, his sister's son, Mordred, would be named as 'Keeper of the Kingdoms' and reign in Britain while Arthur was fighting abroad. Mordred's eventual treachery, which would destroy Arthur and the Round Table, was not foreseen.

The King's helmet was enamelled with silver-edged eye-slits. His gauntlets shone with gold and were edged with pearls and shining stones. He strode to his steed, carrying his broad shield and beautiful mighty sword, Excalibur. Everything flamed red in the early morning sun, and to trumpets they travelled on horses in all their trappings. To cornets and clarions they charged as many bold Lords said goodbye to their lives, sprawled in the mud where all ran red.

Also the bold bowmen of Britain fought against these foot-soldiers from alien lands. The cream of the cavalry on iron-grey horses alighted to heal their wounds with the waters of the magic well. None of the Christian Knights would harm a woman or child, but many brave warriors were butchered and much blood was shed.

When King Arthur returned to Britain he learned of Mordred's treachery and betrayal, and that he had killed the wondrous knight Gawain leaving him in the field, fists full of grass and his sword and shield swimming in blood. Arthur mourned his loss and prayed to a Maiden with an infant in her arms, the most honoured in all heaven. But Arthur's Britain was as much pagan as Christian, and in truth King Arthur himself was invested with the virtues and powers of a pagan god.

Arthur blamed himself and was inconsolable: he swore to avenge the death of Gawain his kinsman. With Geoffrey at the head of his cavalry he killed the treacherous Mordred but was himself fatally wounded, and he was conveyed to mythical Avalon. The days of the fellowship of the Round Table were over, but "A myth is like a monument, its foundations in vanished worlds and its top in worlds to come".

Once a story is tied to a legend it is thought that it could not have actually happened in history – but in fact anything that survives so much time and change must be eternal – and that eternal world can bend the human, mortal world to its own shape. The mythical Arthur is far more important than any real King Arthur. The sun rose on a land without an historical king, but it rose on a land that had created a legend, and the legend was of all time and places. It is the symbolical that generates magic.

Temenos – In Studio Campion
Memories of Visions Past and Present

"Symbols – persons
Live or dead
Assemble, recast
To Act – perform a sleeping play"

Geoffrey Key, 'Dreaming'

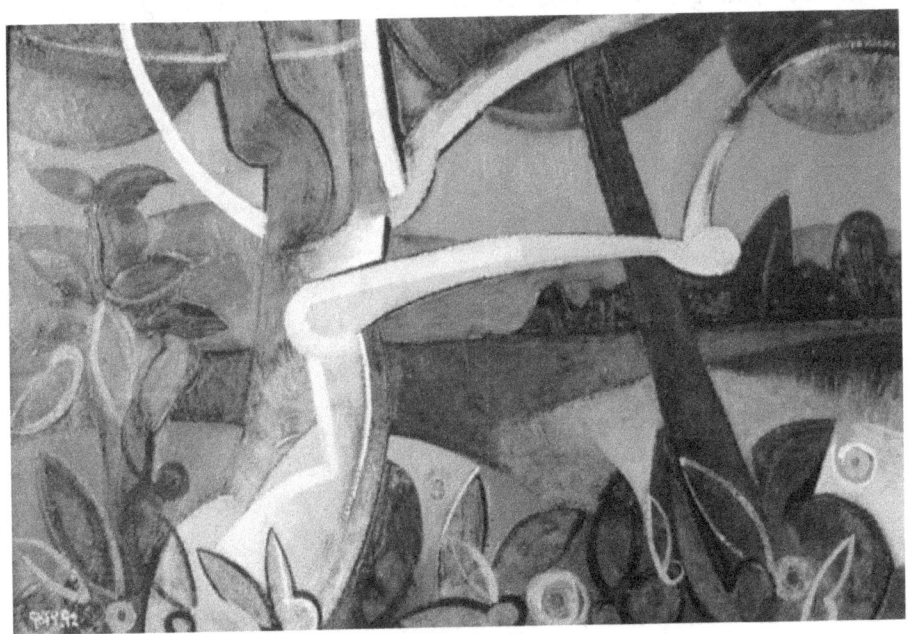

White Tree

Geoffrey always rose very early and dressed immaculately in his elegant clothes before entering his large studio for a day of work. He believed in dedicated application and rarely missed a day at the easel. A few years ago he and his lifelong partner and muse, Eleanor, had moved to this very large house so that Geoffrey would have a much bigger studio and garden. When working he would listen to classical and baroque music; art and music share the same language. There was also an office for Eleanor and endless bookshelves for their huge collection. The books covered the walls and included all her brilliant published volumes of Geoffrey's work. She kept a full data base and documented everything he created; it was the work of decades. Geoffrey revelled in the space and the inspirational view from the windows. With its mixture of artefacts both classical and romantic, his garden was surely Avalon, where King Arthur is said to sleep in a deep cave beneath a white hawthorn tree that blossoms all year.

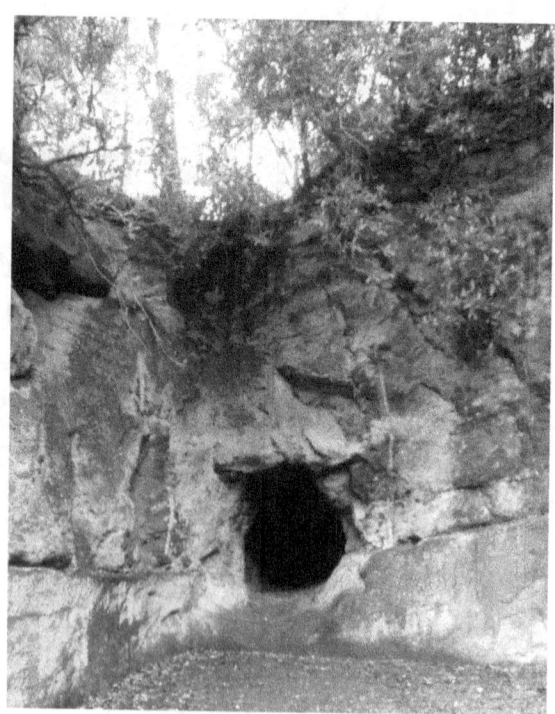

Cave at Alderley Edge

The great painter and sculptor was an imposing, majestic, and charismatic figure, flamboyantly clothed, with beautiful Danish rings of silver and black agate on his expressive fingers. Several fedoras graced the head of one of his carvings, and his multi-coloured shoes were excitingly theatrical. His red, striped and embossed trousers resembled those of the mediaeval German foot-soldiers, the Landsknecht. Downstairs he had a 14th century carving of just such a figure. His long, flowing fair curls and ever-watchful, keenly observant blue eyes gave him a rather Scandinavian appearance. He was brilliant, handsome, and immensely erudite, but had miraculously retained the child's intensity of vision. He had been especially close to his adored mother, who had encouraged his artistic talent from his earliest days. His paintings of equine power in war often included war-chariots. The origin of these remarkable paintings lay in his childhood visits with his mother to the Manchester Art Gallery, and the impact of his small boy's eye-level encounter with the famous 'Chariot Ride' painting. It had felt as though he was directly in the path of the thundering, snorting, open-mouthed horses as they pulled their racing chariots and riders straight towards him. Oh, what fear and excitement, what drama he had felt!

"There are beings in the universe, greater than men and lower than angels. They are known to you, in story and legend, under many names. These beings know the doors between the universes and they have the power to take quiet empty ones where little or nothing is going on, and re-furnish them so to speak..." Geoffrey was undoubtedly one of those rare humans who took his role in these other universes, and imbued his creations with a totemic power. One only had to look at his carvings of Yorick's skull and that of a horse to see the truth of this. Both of these carvings had come from Geoffrey's imagination, but underlaid with knowledge of anatomy, former observations of the real thing, and an understanding of their liminal nature. These things were invisible to ordinary mortals. He took his place in the story of Hamlet and of Passelande, sharing their immortality and vision.

His mother's love for him had felt eternal, and this had always expressed itself in his work as an artist. He had found his own time and place as an artist and in his home environment, but his identity was also miraculously fluid. Through his paintings and sculptures he travelled through time and the Universe. He was one of these rare beings who could see what others could not, and enter the portal to other worlds. His birthday on May 13th coincided with the exquisite flowering of the white hawthorn in its expression of male potency and the power of the white goddess. Also, like the holy Well-Heads, the hawthorn was thought to invite fairies, and stand on the threshold of the Otherworlds. May was Geoffrey's favourite month, and it began with Beltane, a day in celebration of the union between the white goddess and the green man. His paintings of the open-mouthed, leaf-entwined pagan symbol were ravishing. This sacred union between the male and female divine was expressed as Heiros-Gamos, and from their very first meeting and nights on the Nab, belonged to Geoffrey and Eleanor alone. Geoffrey's extraordinarily beautiful Oil Painting "White Tree", in which bodies both masculine and feminine emerged from the tree form is a vision of an erotic consummation between the month of May and that of October, the birth months of Geoffrey and Eleanor. Myths are the seeds of conception;

"Across the shimmering meadows…
Ah, when he came to me!
In the spring-time,
In the night-time,
In the starlight,
Beneath the hawthorn tree."

When on excursions or in his garden looking up at the night sky, Geoffrey felt the power of logic and physics applied to the mysteries of the universe, but also the intoxication and fun of breaking free from those constraining theories. Eleanor must have felt just the same when riding towards the great Jodrell Bank telescope:

"Near Blackden Heath, where people look beyond the stars. Imagine a place where people gather to look at the stars, then look between and beyond, far out into space. We imagined that this must have been going on in places all over our world, for thousands of years. In relatively recent times equipment has been developed and built to help further the distances we can see and measure and so think about - but all the time it's because the place has magic that it is a portal for visionaries."

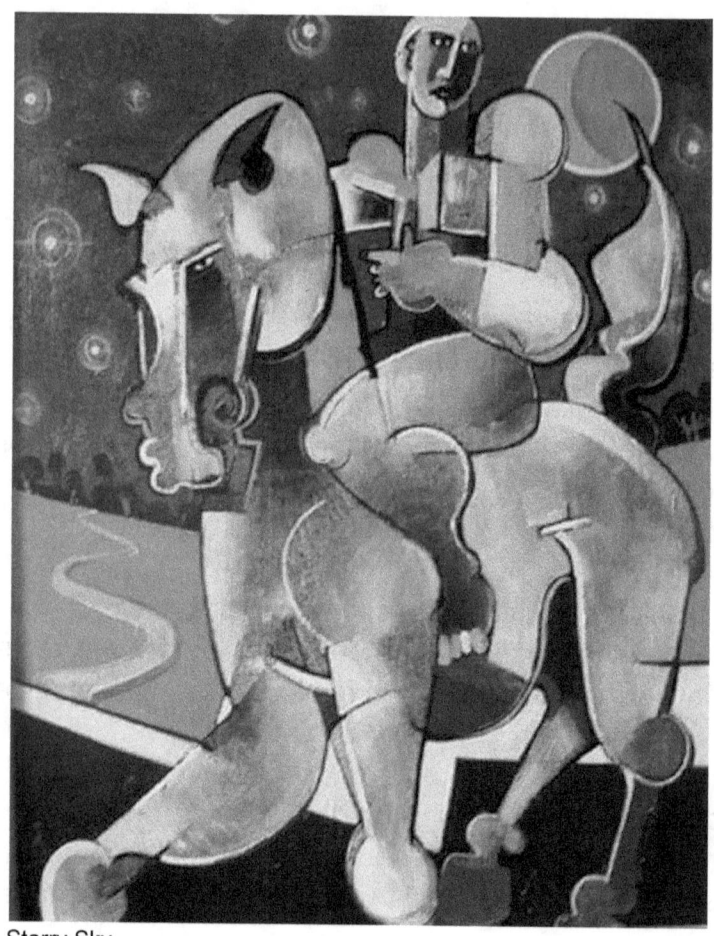

Starry Sky

Geoffrey was fascinated by dream states and what they could reveal to him. Many years previously when out walking on the moors, he had come across a near-derelict Elizabethan Well-House, the waters of which had been thought to possess healing powers to treat diseases of the eye. The ancient Well-Head was cast with a face of a lion, but in his subsequent series of Well-Head paintings, Geoffrey had made the image much more abstracted and geometric. He had always said that it is the structure of the painting and not the subject matter that is of prime importance to him. In all the marvellous Well-Head series of paintings the Well-Head itself appears as an ancient myth-laden portal to another world or universe. Entry is through the eyes and the open mouth speaks of a creator who has lived many times. Looking at this series is like an encounter with the Oracle at Delphi, or the bones of a beloved ancestor. Geoffrey's night-riders, abstract or fully figurative, gazing up at the moon or starlit heavens, resemble primeval or mediaeval astronomers, able to see far more deeply than their modern counterparts.

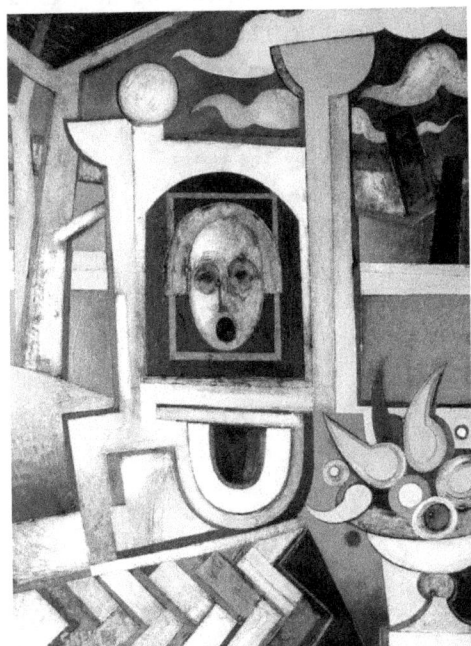

Well Head

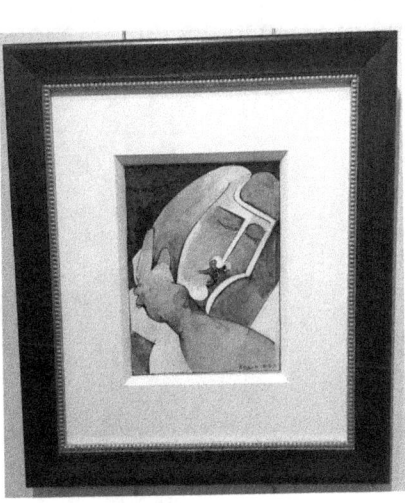

Sleeping Head

The most recent project with his partner Eleanor, whom he had first drawn from the shadows on the Nab to become his 'perfect light', had been the creation of a majestic book with the title 'Infinite Jest'. It documented his creation over many years of jesters and clowns, and the many figures associated with the Commedia del Arte. Throughout all his life he had loved jesters, but had been very afraid of clowns. The cap and bells, and multi-coloured, geometric costumes of jesters were immensely appealing, but the clowns he had encountered as a very small child, taken to the circus by his grandparents, had terrified him. His great trait of observation had been with him all his life, and was apparent as a very young child. The jester image seemed to have been in his imagination for as long as he could remember.

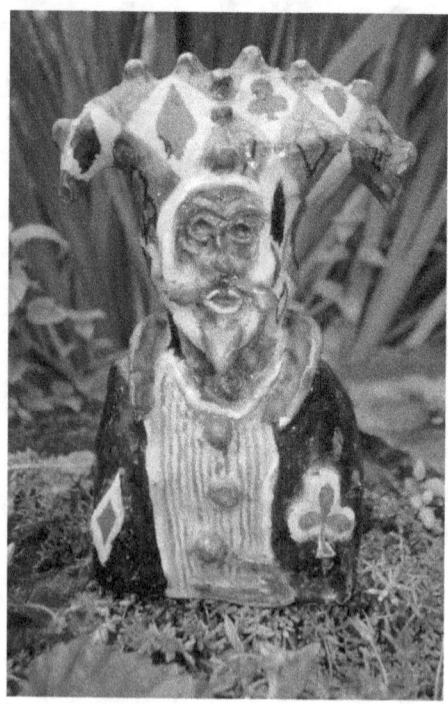

Ceramic Jester

At the age of eleven, he made a ceramic jester, which now lives in his kitchen. He was infected with a love of jester imagery which has remained with him always – those wonderful decorative costumes, masks, and headgear.

> "Jesters of the Past
> Develop in the Mind
> And Pass Onto
> The Foolscap of Today"

Clowns were a very different matter for the young Geoffrey. They appeared frequently in the circus that was staged in the park opposite his childhood home. He loathed the noise, and chaos of the clowns, and their grotesque make-up. For Geoffrey, they were the stuff of nightmares, and his clown series of 2001 might be regarded as a way of tackling those early demons.

> "The clowns appear
> Their grotesque dress and mask
> Make me look away and hide
> Just Old Men with painted faces
> Let me see the horses
> And the spangled ladies"

The many works documented and illustrated in the book 'Infinite Jest' had laid many demons to rest, through the paintings of clowns and jesters. The carved, wooden 'Yorick's Skull' had expressed his love for the plays of Shakespeare, especially Hamlet. Geoffrey felt that fully realised works of art perhaps created their own universes, and maybe 'Infinite Jest', the book itself, had brought into being a separate universe into which he could travel. He felt that both he and Eleanor had knowledge of the ways between the worlds. The horse skull in Eleanor's office, which she kept on a bookshelf, was thought to have an apotropaic function, protecting the owner from evil. He smiled to himself when he remembered that Denmark like Cheshire and Lancashire was a land of bogs, wooded and watery, liminal places where worlds were said to overlap and intersect. And Hamlet's Kronborg castle at Elsinore had its own legend of the sleeping warrior, entombed beneath the earth. Like King Arthur and Charlemagne, Holger the Dane was said to be seated on a rock throne beneath Kronborg, and if Denmark is ever in trouble and has need of a hero, then he will wake from his long sleep and defend her. It was yet another luminous legend, but also darkly foreboding, like many of Geoffrey's sculptures. The artist was undoubtedly godlike in that he could draw images from the mind and imagination and thus give birth to another world. Geoffrey was primarily a classicist but also a romantic. Like a necromancer amidst his own enchantments he conjured worlds and brought them into being. His power was transformative. "There never was such an artist on this earth, nor ever will be again."

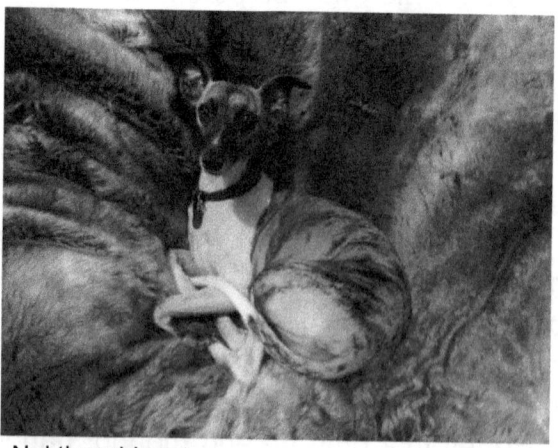

Nel the whippet

Eleanor was out riding her horse Albion on Alderley Edge, one of the many places that claimed to hold the sleeping King Arthur and his Knights. Recently, a number of writers had aggressively asserted the historical veracity of a Northern Arthur, Gogledd – hero of the Old North, whilst counter-claims for Cornwall and Wales were voiced with equal passion and certainty. This regional bias actually related to the non-historical material concerning Arthur. It seemed obvious to Geoffrey that Arthur was a King for all times and places, and could not be confined to one location. He was an archetype. Just as the practitioners of so called 'Northern Art' had frequently migrated to Cornwall, or painted subjects that either had no regional connection, or were products of the imagination, so Arthur had journeyed in all places. By trying to pigeonhole Arthur into a particular area of the country, they missed the point entirely and failed to understand the meaning and power of myth. Like the endless Lowry imitators there was now a 'monstrous Regiment of Arthurs.'

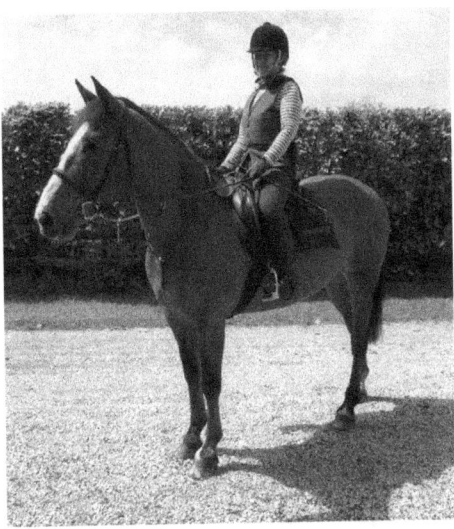

Eleanor on Albion

Geoffrey almost always painted thematically, and his current series 'gastronomic' celebrated the joy of kitchens, food and wine. He had always loved fine dining and now that his work for the day was completed, he looked forward to the Home Universe of sharing a meal and bottle of Tarlant champagne with Eleanor, then cuddling up on the sofa with their adorable whippet, Nel.

At that moment, as he was descending the stairs, he heard the key turn in the door. It was his returning rider.

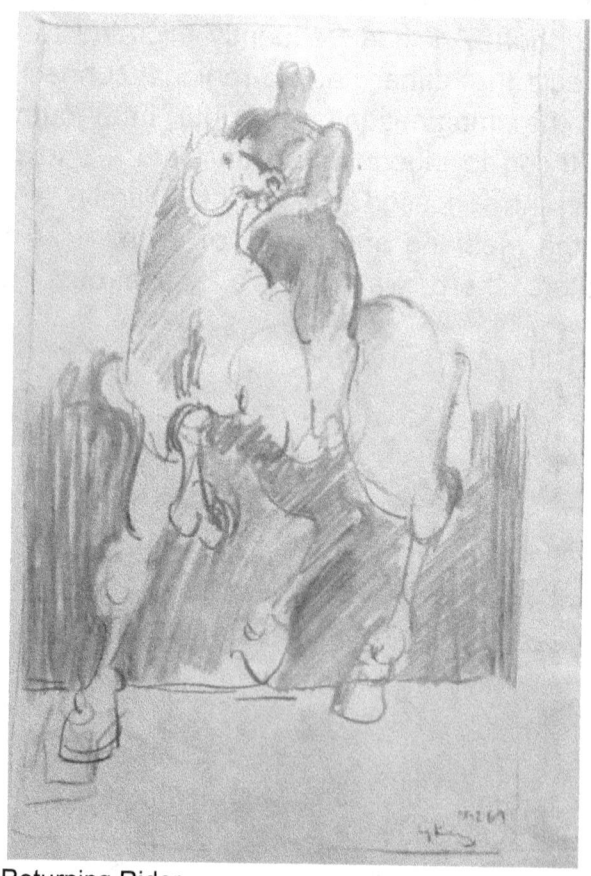

Returning Rider

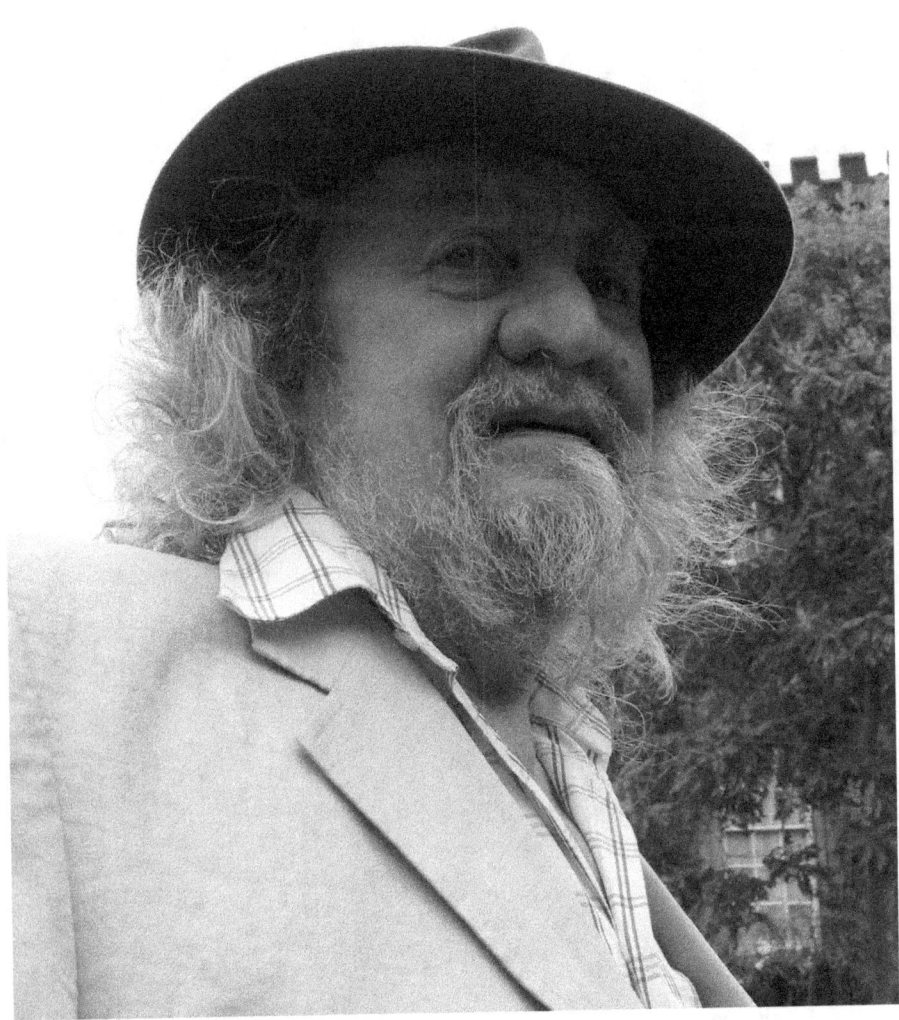
Geoffrey Key

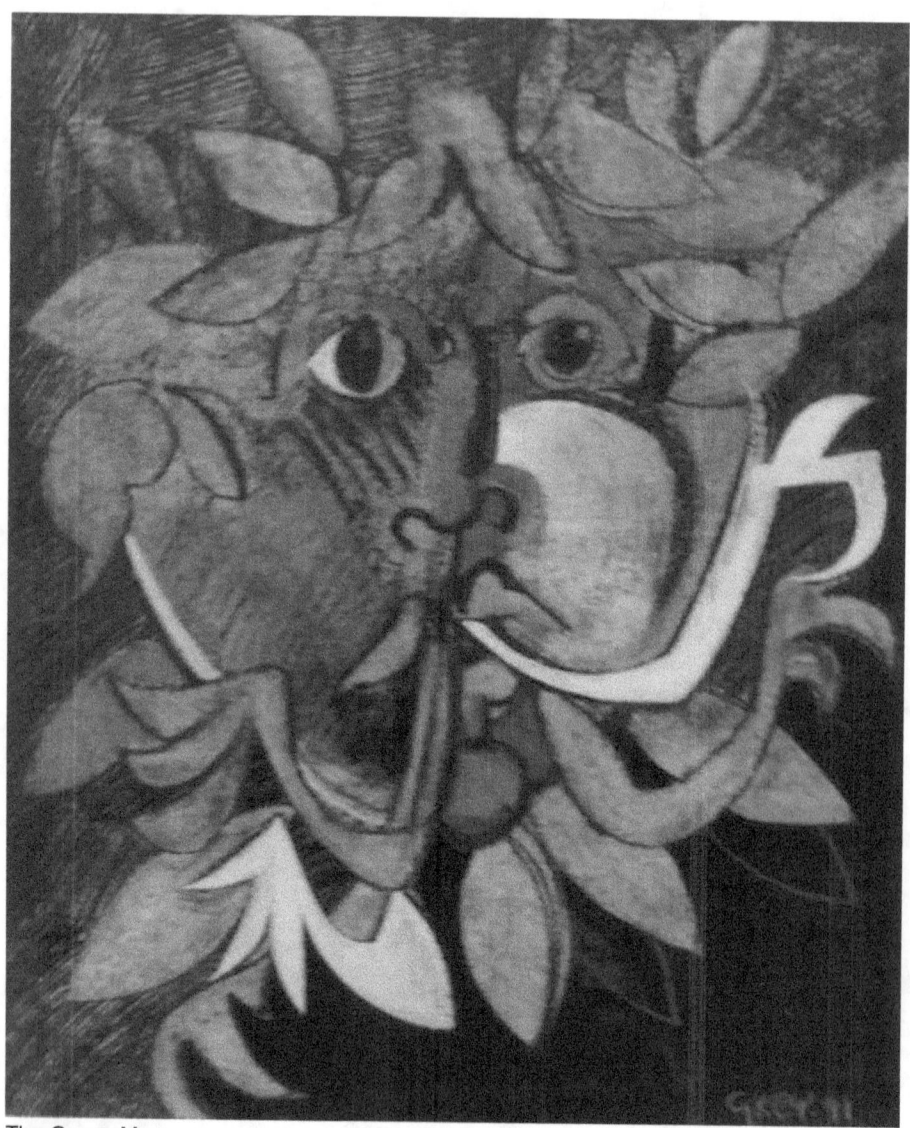

The Green Man

The purpose of this piece is to deepen and further an understanding of Geoffrey's work. The Arthurian myth allows us to act inside the artist's paintings and sculptures; myths are the seeds of conception.

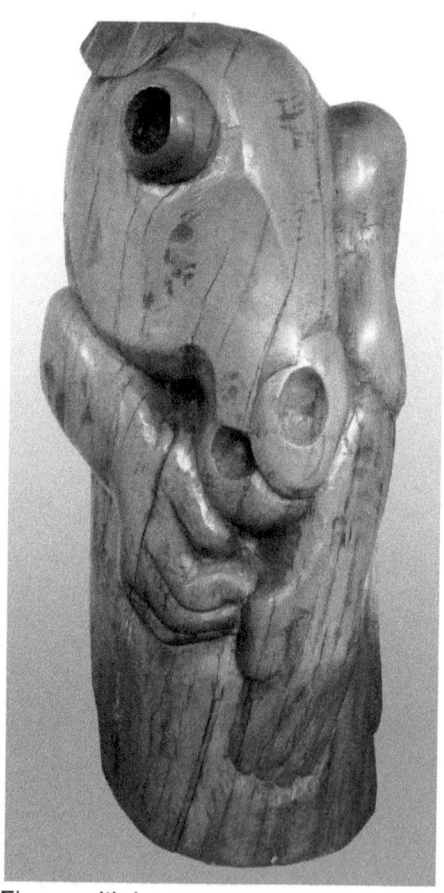

Figure with horse